GERMINATOR

TRICIA HOLDERMAN

THE GERM GIRL'S GUIDE TO
SIMPLE SOLUTIONS
IN A GERM-FILLED WORLD

Advantage.

Published by Advantage, Charleston, South Carolina.
Member of Advantage Media Group.

ADVANTAGE is a registered trademark, and the Advantage colophon is a trademark of Advantage Media Group, Inc.

Printed in the United States of America.

10 9 8 7 6 5 4 3 2 1

ISBN: 978-1-64225-301-6
LCCN: 2021917017

Cover design by Analisa Smith.
Interior design by Wesley Strickland.

This publication is designed to provide accurate and authoritative information in regard to the subject matter covered. It is sold with the understanding that the publisher is not engaged in rendering legal, accounting, or other professional services. If legal advice or other expert assistance is required, the services of a competent professional person should be sought.

Advantage Media Group is proud to be a part of the Tree Neutral® program. Tree Neutral offsets the number of trees consumed in the production and printing of this book by taking proactive steps such as planting trees in direct proportion to the number of trees used to print books. To learn more about Tree Neutral, please visit **www.treeneutral.com**.

Advantage Media Group is a publisher of business, self-improvement, and professional development books and online learning. We help entrepreneurs, business leaders, and professionals share their Stories, Passion, and Knowledge to help others Learn & Grow. Do you have a manuscript or book idea that you would like us to consider for publishing? Please visit **advantagefamily.com** or call **1.866.775.1696**.

This book is dedicated to Wes and Theresa. I could never accomplish all that I do without you!

Thank you to all those I have learned from and taught over the years in the quest to conquer germs.

CONTENTS

INTRODUCTION

The COVID-19 pandemic got a lot of people thinking about germs, maybe for the first time ever. Suddenly, every other person you meet is a clean freak. People who never knew infection prevention was a thing were suddenly spraying their groceries with disinfectant and walking around in homemade hazmat suits. Some even invested (and are still investing) in expensive equipment like water ionizers and air filtration systems to keep their homes germ-free. And while that might sound extreme, it's not a crazy impulse. This pandemic will certainly end at some point and may even be

Health crises are predictable and cyclical, but we can all learn to prepare for them.

over by the time you pick up this book. Health crises are predictable and cyclical, but we can all learn to prepare for them.

That's where I come in.

I've always been a little obsessed with cleanliness. When I was seventeen and teaching aerobics to make money for college, I cleaned all the mirrors and equipment in between classes. And I was good at it! One of the ladies in one of my classes was so impressed with my cleaning abilities, she asked me if I would clean her house. When I found out it paid five times as much as teaching aerobics, I was in. Forty-two years later, what started as a summer job is now a corporation that has two regional branches and handles infection prevention for major hospitals, NFL and NBA teams and arenas, and countless large and small businesses and luxury homes across the country.

Which makes me kind of like the Germinator.

However, the thing that took me to the top of my field wasn't my ability to produce a smudge-free mirror; it was my health. In my twenties, I was diagnosed with Crohn's disease and landed in the hospital with sepsis, which, in case you aren't aware, is the body's extreme response to an infection. For the next three years, I was in and out of the hospital, undergoing something like forty surgeries and suffering several more infections. And I started asking myself, *Are there things I could do as a patient that could prevent these infections?* The answer was obviously yes, but, as the head of a business that specialized in cleaning, stuck in a hospital bed with nothing more to do than look around, I also noticed some things about my environment that I thought needed to be brought to somebody's attention.

For example, my IV pole—it was covered with fingerprints and had dust on the top, which was a red flag that maybe I was not in an environment where cleanliness was a top priority. Trust me, if it's not visually clean, it can't possibly be clean. Plus, I couldn't understand the rationale behind which surfaces were being cleaned versus the ones not being cleaned. They changed my sheets every day, which was totally unnecessary, but almost never wiped down the table over my bed. The bathroom was given a sort of wipe down, but there was no actual cleaning going on. And this was happening in a hospital, where unsanitary conditions might really *kill* somebody.

So I learned everything I could about infection prevention, basically as a matter of survival. This was back in the eighties when disinfecting was just bleach and water being wiped on everything. I got involved in the development of new, safer, more effective cleaning solutions and was named to Procter and Gamble's advisory board for commercial products when I was just thirty-three years old—something that pretty much never happens. And I didn't get there because I have a PhD in infection prevention from some university. There is no degree in infection prevention, not on the human side and not on the facility side. And there's certainly no single, reliable place for a person who hasn't spent forty-two years in the cleaning business to turn for information (and a lot of the information out there is terrible!). While I do have a Certificate of Mastery in Infection Prevention, everything I know I've pieced together on my own, through years of hands-on experience, self-guided study, and, as I mentioned, earning my CMIP. And I know a lot—so much I could write a book on infection prevention … which you happen to be reading.

Over the next nine brief chapters, I will share things I know and things you need to know to keep yourself and your loved ones safe from germs, both inside your home and out in the world. You'll learn what germs really are, where they linger and how they spread, and the most effective ways to get rid of them before they get to you. You'll learn what you need to buy and do to keep

Ready? Let's go bust some germs.

your house not just clean but also sanitary—and what is a waste of your money and time. And you'll learn how to keep yourself safe when you leave your home to shop, work, travel, and interact with the rest of the world—including if, like me, you ever find yourself in the hospital.

Ready? Let's go bust some germs.

Note: CMIP is a certification earned from the Association for the Health Care Environment (AHE), a Professional Membership Group of the American Hospital Association.

CHAPTER 1:

GERMS, GERMS, GERMS

T his whole book is dedicated to one thing: fighting germs. But what exactly is a germ, besides something you can't see that can somehow get inside you and make you sick? "Germ" is actually a catchall term that applies to three different types of organisms that can mess with your health: bacteria, fungi, and viruses. Let's look at them one at a time.

Bacteria

Bacteria are the most common germs. They're one-celled organisms that feed off of their environment—and if you've ever had strep throat or a cavity in your tooth, you know that that environment can be *you*. However, bacteria don't need a host like a human, animal, or plant to survive. They can live basically anywhere—in the water we drink, the air we breathe, the dirt on the ground, as well as in your carpet, your furniture, and even your body. They also reproduce quickly; for example, *E. coli* reproduces every twenty minutes!

Most bacteria aren't as dangerous as *E. coli*. In fact, plenty of them are necessary for good health. So-called "good bacteria," found naturally in your body, help you digest food, provide necessary vitamins, and fight off harmful bacteria. It's those harmful bacteria that we need to stay away from—those bacteria produce toxins that make you sick or invade healthy tissue. In addition to *E. coli*, they include things like anthrax and staphylococcus, which causes potentially deadly staph infections, as well as more common conditions like ear infections and UTIs. They can be transmitted both directly, by ingesting or breathing them, and indirectly—and can survive on surfaces for days or even months.

Fungi

When you hear the word "fungi," you might think of mushrooms, or if you're a serious foodie, maybe even truffles. But not all fungi can be found on a restaurant menu. While most of them are harmless, including some that exist naturally in the body, there are other fungi that can make you sick. Think yeast infections, candida, mold allergies, and athlete's foot.

Fungi are primitive, multicelled organisms that feed on soil, plants, and animals and thrive in damp, warm environments. They reproduce by spreading microscopic spores, and those spores are what make you sick when they are inhaled or come into contact with the skin. People with healthy immune systems can usually fight fungal infections off easily, but they can be serious, especially to people with weakened immune systems from conditions like cancer or HIV. Fungi are also the hardiest of all the germs—some fungi spores can live on a surface like a piece of glass (or your bathroom tile) for *years*. Which is just scary.

Viruses

Viruses are the smallest germs. They aren't even a whole cell, just some DNA or RNA in a protein coating, and can't survive without a host, like an animal, a plant, or you. However, as the recent COVID-19 pandemic has proven, when they

Unlike bacteria and fungi, there are no "good" viruses.

find a human host, they can reproduce quickly and pack quite a punch. And unlike bacteria and fungi, there are no "good" viruses. There are only things like norovirus (a viral stomach bug), chicken pox, measles, mumps, hepatitis, herpes, HIV/AIDS, and even the common flu.

Viruses are dangerous because they are so easily transmissible. They can be transmitted through inhalation, orally, and through contact with feces, surfaces, and even dust. Hardier viruses like HIV can be transmitted through blood, secretions, or organ transplants. However, because they need a host to survive, they can only survive on surfaces for a period of time.

How long do germs live on the most common surfaces in our lives? Here's a brief rundown:

LIFE OF A GERM
WITHOUT PROPER CLEANING

SURFACES/MATERIALS	VIRUS CORONA, HIV/ AIDS, CHICKEN POX, MEASLES/MUMPS, NOROVIRUS, HERPES	BACTERIA UTIS, MRSA, E-COLI, C-DIFF, STAPH, EAR ACHES, TB, ANTHRAX	FUNGI ATHLETE'S FOOT, MENINGITIS, CANDIDA, YEAST INFECTION, MOLD ALLERGIES
PLASTICS: CREDIT CARDS, KEYBOARDS, KEY CARDS/BADGES	4 DAYS	60-90 DAYS	90+ DAYS
METALS: DOOR HANDLES, CELL PHONES, JEWELRY	3 DAYS	60-70 DAYS	90+ DAYS
WOOD: FURNITURE, COUNTERTOPS, CUTTING BOARDS	4 DAYS	40 DAYS	1-2 YEARS
PAPER/CARDBOARD: BOXES, MAIL, TOILET PAPER	24 DAYS	UP TO 72 HOURS	INDEFINITE
CLOTH/LEATHER: PURSE, UPHOLSTERY, CARPET, STEERING WHEEL	3 DAYS	9 WEEKS - 7 MONTHS	INDEFINITE
STONE: SHOWER TILES, COUNTERS, FLOORS	3 DAYS	60 DAYS	INDEFINITE
GLASS: DISHES, MIRRORS, WINDOWS, CELL PHONE, FACE	4-7 DAYS	10-14 DAYS	1-3 MONTHS

So now you know what germs are, where you can find them, how long they can hang around, and how they get into your body. In the next chapter, we'll start exploring how to get rid of them before they're transmitted by taking a closer look at the different types of cleaning.

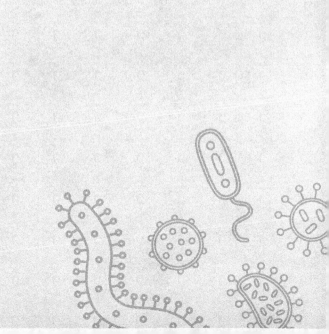

CHAPTER 2:

HOW CLEAN IS CLEAN?

E verybody has a different idea of clean. Some people insist on having floors so sparkly and shiny, you could eat off of them. Others are fine as long as their house doesn't smell bad, and they can make it from the living room to the bathroom without tripping over something. And some

Clean tends to be a matter of opinion.

people ... well, they might not even go that far. Clean tends to be a matter of opinion.

But when it comes to infection prevention, cleaning is all about facts. In the introduction, I mentioned that if something doesn't look clean, it

Just because something looks clean doesn't mean it's germ-free. can't possibly be clean. However, the opposite, unfortunately, isn't true. Just because something looks clean doesn't mean it's germ-free. There are specific things that cleaning needs to accomplish to create a safe, healthy environment. Those are the things I'm talking about when I say the word "clean."

I divide cleaning into four basic categories: cleaning, disinfecting, sanitizing, and sterilizing.

Cleaning

Cleaning is essentially the removal of dirt from surfaces—getting jelly off the floor, getting blood off a bedrail, things of that sort. Vacuuming carpets, sweeping floors, dusting furniture, and wiping off countertops all constitute cleaning. On its own, cleaning helps a home or business or other location look, smell, and even feel its best. However, when it comes to removing germs from the environment, cleaning alone is not enough to actually make a place safe. For that, you need to add the following:

DISINFECTING

Disinfecting is the chemical process of killing germs—usually by applying some sort of spray or liquid solution to them. It won't get the jelly off of the floor or the blood off of the bedrail; however, it will kill any bacteria or viruses and some fungi in that jelly or blood, so they can't make you sick. Obviously, that's not enough for most people either, so they tend to combine cleaning with disinfecting by spraying a disinfecting cleaner on whatever they want to clean and then wiping it off. When done properly (more on that later), this process makes whatever surface you clean as clean as it looks.

SANITIZING

Sanitizing is the reduction of the number of germs to a safe level. It is mostly used in food preparation areas and refers to eliminating or reducing bacteria by disinfecting. What is considered a safe level depends on public health standards or requirements at a workplace, school, etc. What you do to sanitize will vary, depending on your needs. For example, you sanitize your hands, but you should never use disinfectant on your skin, only sanitizer designed specifically for that purpose. Disinfectant is too strong and will eventually damage skin in addition to killing germs.

STERILIZING

Sterilizing takes disinfecting to the next level by adding heat. Most germs will die if heated to a certain temperature—for example, most viruses die at 160 degrees. So sterilization happens in a lot of professional settings, like hospitals and dental offices, where people would otherwise be more exposed to germs (like on the utensils the dentist uses in your mouth— you definitely don't want someone else's germs on those!). Chemicals can also be combined to be used for sanitization when heat is not the best option, like in some industrial-strength cleaning chemicals.

At home, most people don't really need to sterilize much of anything, although your dishwasher probably gets hot enough to sterilize your dishes. A hired carpet or upholstery cleaner may also sterilize your furniture or rugs, but that's about the limit for at-home sterilization. If your goal is to keep your home safe and germ-free, you really don't need it. A regular combination of cleaning and disinfecting should be more than enough to keep you and your loved ones safe. We'll take a closer look at the different chemicals you can use for the job in the next chapter.

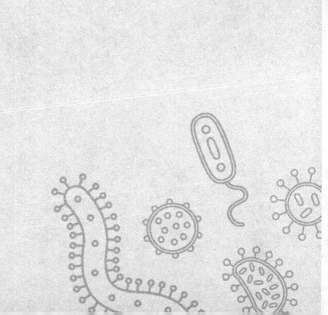

CHAPTER 3:

THE CHEMISTRY OF CLEAN

All cleaning chemicals are not the same—but most people don't know that. And the result can be dangerous. I've seen this over and over, but the most recent example that sticks out was a visit to one of my corporate clients during the pandemic. This was a law firm with a very elegant, fancy office—far too elegant, in the office manager's mind, for there to be plastic bottles of disinfectant sitting around everywhere. That would be tacky. Instead, there were lovely glass dispenser bottles of a bright blue liquid strategically positioned around the office.

Now, I've been a cleaning professional for a long time, and I have never in my life seen a disinfectant in such a beautiful, bright shade of blue. So I asked the office manager where this disinfectant came from.

You need the right chemical for the right purpose.

She showed me a big bottle of toilet bowl cleaner.

In other words, it was *acid*. But the word "disinfectant" was on the label.

No wonder the carpet under the dispenser bottles was discolored.

The moral of the story is that it's not enough to just squirt a chemical on something and expect it to safely kill all the germs. You need the right chemical for the right purpose. This chapter will help you choose wisely—and save your surfaces from acid attacks.

These are the different types of cleaners:

Disinfectants

Disinfectants are the most common cleaners that regular consumers use—they're the popular, brand-name and generic cleaners you see lining the shelves. They usually come in the form of aerosol sprays, disinfecting spray cleaners, and disinfecting wipes. Many of these products now claim to kill both bacteria and viruses, and most also kill fungi.

Antimicrobial Barriers

An antimicrobial barrier is applied by wiping or spraying the chemical on a surface. The chemical leaves behind a coating that inhibits the growth of germs by starving them to death.

Bleach

Back in the day, before all these fancy cleaning products were invented, people just used bleach and water to disinfect their homes. Which was both good and bad. On the good side, bleach kills *everything*. On the not-so-good side, that everything includes things you don't want to kill, like your clothing, your plants, or anything bleach might come into contact with. Bleach is so caustic it can be a health hazard, especially to people with respiratory issues like asthma or COPD. This is why they stopped (with a few exceptions) using it to clean in hospitals.

"Green" Disinfectants

I put the word "green" in quotes for a reason—there is no such thing as a green disinfectant, at least not yet. Yes, there are plenty of so-called green disinfectants on the shelf right next to the other disinfecting products. Unfortunately, they are not technically disinfectants, because anything that is green cannot kill. This is not to say you shouldn't use green cleaners, only that you should use them under the right circumstances.

How Do You Choose Which Chemical to Use?

There are so many specialized cleaners out there, you might be surprised that I only have five cleaners in my house—and one of them is a vinegar vegetable wash. The other four that I use for general cleaning are:

1. A disinfectant
2. A general or neutral cleaner
3. Dishwashing soap
4. Toilet bowl cleaner

That's it. So my basic advice, if your goal is simple cleanliness, picking up dust or grime or whatever with a general cleaner or even a green cleaner is fine. If you want to polish or make something shiny, you can use a glass cleaner. Simple dishwashing soap is perfect for most dining tables for removing germs and debris. As for removing germs from the air with an aerosol disinfectant, you really only need to do that when other people come into your home (and in your car, but we'll get to that later).

If your goal is to kill germs from something like raw chicken that was on your countertop, you want to be sure to use a real disinfectant, and you want to use it in a very specific way. A lot of people don't realize that when you spray a disinfectant cleaner, you need to wait before you wipe. Most chemicals need at least sixty seconds to three or four minutes in order to be totally effective and kill everything that you want to kill. This is called a **dwell time**, referring to the amount of time a chemical needs to "dwell" on a surface to do its job.

This also means spray cleaners are much more effective than cleaning wipes. While wipes may contain the same disinfecting solution as a spray, when you use a wipe, you're wiping the chemical away before it has time to do its job. Plus, most wipes do not stay wet long enough to kill most of the germs.

One final word on disinfecting surfaces—if you're cleaning up something like raw chicken, you need to disinfect the entire countertop, not just the general area where the chicken was. Even when you think the germs are contained to one spot, germ spores have the ability to spread out where you can't see them. So remove everything from the counter, spray your disinfectant cleaner over the entire counter, wait, then wipe it all off. Then wipe down whatever you took off the counter before you put it back.

A Word about Dilutable Chemicals

Especially since the COVID-19 pandemic, a lot of people have been buying professional-strength, dilutable chemical cleaners online. These are chemicals you mix with water, and there are usually instructions as to how much water to use. Unfortunately, not everyone follows directions. If the label says the ratio should be one part chemical to eight parts water, you don't want to be one of those people who thinks,

There's not a whole lot of point in cleaning something if you're just going to destroy it!

Hey, if eight-to-one is good, maybe one-to-one is better! I promise you, it's not. If you want to get scientific about it, a solution's effectiveness is more about dwell time than about strength.

More importantly, you don't want to ruin whatever surface you're putting the chemical on. There's not a whole lot of point in cleaning something if you're just going to destroy it!

This should give you a clearer idea of the chemicals you need to keep your home clean and germ-free. In the next chapter, we'll look at the right equipment to use with and without those chemicals.

CHAPTER 4:

TOOLS OF THE TRADE

What tools should you have on hand to keep your house germ-free, and which ones are doing more harm than good? This chapter will help you build the most effective arsenal for your germ-busting endeavors.

Wipes and Rags

We talked about wet wipes in the last chapter—and why they aren't my favorite tool for disinfecting or cleaning. I do use them when I'm away from home, but inside my house, I use plain old microfiber wipers to clean just about every surface. Wipes and rags can be anything from microfibers to disposable or minimal-use wipes that you buy at the grocery store to old T-shirts or towels that you repurpose. I prefer microfiber towels because they have thousands and thousands of tiny little pieces of looped material that grab whatever you're cleaning and lift it up. With a T-shirt, when you're wiping stuff, you're truly just moving those germs back and forth. I also prefer reusable wipers because, when I'm done with them, I can throw them in the washing machine.

Dusters

The old-fashioned image of the maid with the feather duster isn't just out of date; it doesn't actually work. Feathers are not effective when it comes to removing dust. They are only effective at moving it around. If you want a "duster on a stick" that you can use on delicate things or things that are out of reach, a better bet is a duster with a removable, microfiber head. These come in both disposable and washable varieties.

Sponges and Scrubbers

I don't know where people get the idea that sponges are meant to be reused and reused and reused. In fact, I don't think sponges should be used at all. I don't allow anyone on my staff to use a sponge, ever, and my advice to you is not to use them either. The way sponges are designed to stay wet and slowly dry out makes them a breeding ground for bacteria. A wiper is fine for most kitchen jobs (just remember to throw it in the washer when you're done), or, if you need something to scrub your dishes or other surfaces, one of those green scrubbers without the sponge part works great. And if, for some reason, you can't let go of your sponge, do not use it to clean up raw meat or anything else that might harbor bacteria.

Mops

Look in most anyone's garage and you'll likely find one of those old-fashioned mops that looks like a sheepdog. When I see them, it just scares me to death. Those mops are not only breeding grounds for germs, but the other problem is, when you use one and hang it out to dry, some of the dirt stays behind, even if you rinse it off. The next time you get the mop wet, you wind up smearing that old dirt on your floor. I'm also not fond of sponge mops. There's not really a good way to launder them to kill the germs from what they pick up.

I'm a big fan of microfiber mops—the flat ones with the removable microfiber pads, because I can wash them after I use them. Flat mops with disposable pads are also good, because you throw the pad away when you're finished with it. Some come with pads that are presoaked in disinfectant, and for those that aren't, you can add your own (appropriate!) cleaner. Just remember to allow for the necessary dwell times.

My floors are as important as my countertops, so each time I clean them, I want to start with a fresh mop, and microfiber lets me do that. I also love that microfiber mops are flat, so I can clean without moving the dirt around (more on that later) and throw them in the washing machine when I'm finished cleaning. That said, I don't need my floors to be so clean I can eat off of them. No one does. Your feet go on the floor, and it's impossible to keep your feet disinfected all the time. So there is no five-second rule in my house—if food falls on the floor, it goes in the trash. That way I can use a neutral cleaner on my floors that won't damage the surface and won't hurt my pets.

Vacuums

I use a vacuum for everything. My house is about 50 percent carpet and 50 percent tile, but I vacuum everything because I want to get every little thing off the floor. My grout stays cleaner because nothing's getting ground into it—I vacuum, then mop, knowing I've removed everything.

Nonbrush vacuums are best for flat floors, which are the woods, the tiles, the marbles, and vinyl. The only thing I would suggest using brushes on is carpeting. I'm ambivalent on rugs, because the beaters on some vacuums tend to be too strong for thinner rugs.

I use a cheap little stick vacuum for my ceramic floors, and I use a HEPA-filtered vacuum for my carpet. The reason? I don't really need the big vacuum with the little brush thing going around for my floors, but on the carpet I do. If you have a pet that sheds, consider a vacuum that is designed to pick up pet hair. These are vacuums that have longer brushes, bigger canisters for holding the hair, and nonclogging hoses. That said, it's not necessary to invest a ton of money in a vacuum. I think the midrange ones work well.

Air Purifiers/Ionizers

Air purifiers and ionizers kill the germs that are floating around in the air. Believe it or not, the dust you can see floating around when the sun comes through the window actually carries germs, and air purifiers and ionizers get rid of them in different ways. Air purifiers use filters, including HEPA filters, which are a web of fibers that trap dust particles as they are sucked into the machine. Ionizers use an electric charge to kill the germs on the dust particles.

The mistake most people make with air purifiers is they think they can put one in one room, and it will purify the air in the entire house. Most air purifiers only cover a limited area—the product information will tell you how many square feet a machine will cover, as well as how frequently that air is being moved. Do your math before you buy to make sure what you bring home is worth the investment.

Water Systems

More and more of my clients are investing in water filtration systems, which get particles out of water, and water ionization systems, which purify water with an electric charge. Ionizing water is somewhat expensive, but more and more people are investing in home ionization systems that can be installed under a faucet, partially because the ionized water can be used for drinking but can also be used as a disinfectant. Unfortunately, on the cleaning side, ionized water is not effective unless you use it right away. The electricity part tapers off quickly, and you end up with just plain water.

I have a water filter on my refrigerator that does awesome work, and that's all I need. I'm not one of those people who needs my water to be absolutely 100 percent pure, but I have done tests on the water in my house, and it's pretty darn close. Portable filter pitchers also work well.

That's a basic overview of the tools you might use to keep your house germ-free. In the next chapter, I'll tell you how to combine those tools with the chemicals we looked at in the previous chapter to get the cleanest, most germ-free home possible.

CHAPTER 5:

HOUSECLEANING 101

s there a right way to clean? As a cleaning professional, I believe there is. It's kind of difficult to explain in writing, but I'll give it a shot.

In cleaning, the goal is to get the dirt off a surface, not move it around. But moving dirt around is what happens when most people clean, because they just wipe in circles, or mop back and forth over the same area—which just spreads the dirt all over the surface. Instead, I use what I call **leading-edge cleaning**. Leading edge kind of means what it sounds like—after first clearing everything off the surface you're cleaning, you always lead with the same edge of your mop, rag

> In cleaning, the goal is to get the dirt off a surface, not move it around.

or whatever you're using and always move forward, pushing the dirt away from the surface you've already cleaned. This method is my secret to cleaning everything from floors to countertops to mirrors and windows.

I realize that may not make a lot of sense in words, so I made a quick video to demonstrate exactly how it works. To check out leading-edge cleaning in action, just go to triciaholderman.com.

How Often Should I Clean?

Cleaning schedules are based on a variety of things, like how many people live in your house, how old you and any other residents are, if there are pets, etc. I set up what's called a maintenance schedule for my clients based on their specific needs—for example, if a client has four pets and three kids in their house, their surfaces are going to need more frequent cleaning than a single person with no pets and no kids.

I clean my house once a week. I do general cleaning—I mop my floors once a week, I vacuum once a week, I clean the bathroom once a week. I do spray my shower with disinfectant almost every day, but that's because, in my business, I enter a lot of different environments where I might be exposed to germs. Most people will be fine with a good weekly cleaning, although if you use bath products that leave behind oils or soap scum, you might want to do it more often.

I clean my kitchen every day, but I don't think that's feasible for everybody—and frankly, if it was feasible, I would be out of business. Most people are good about picking up after themselves in the kitchen and loading dishwashers as needed.

High-Touch versus Low-Touch

I clean the surfaces in my house—like countertops, walls, baseboards, light switches, etc.—based on whether they are "high-touch" or "low-touch" surfaces. Logically, the more often you touch something, the more often you should clean it. So the surfaces in your house that get used over and over, like the light switch you touch every time you walk in the house, or that kitchen counter (that you should clean every time you put chicken on it) should be cleaned at least once a week. Whereas for the light switch in my guest bedroom, which is usually empty, I clean maybe once a year, unless a guest actually stays in the room, in which case I would clean that light switch after the visit.

A Little More on Floors

I once went to a potential client's house to look at her marble floor—the previous housekeeper, who obviously didn't know what she was doing, had decided all the little gray streaks in this woman's very expensive, white marble floor were dirt and therefore needed to be bleached out. The harsh cleaner she used to remove the veins in the marble ate away at the floor, and it cost the poor woman $17,000 to replace it!

The moral of this story is, again, make sure you're using the right products on your floor. I only use neutral products on floors unless my client has a special need for something stronger. Unless you make a habit of eating off of your floor, you don't!

Hopefully, you now have a better idea of how to properly clean your house to keep it germ-free. In the next chapter, we'll deal with how to keep germs at bay when you leave your home and enter the outside world.

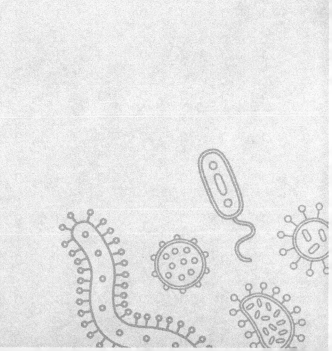

CHAPTER 6:

THE OUTSIDE WORLD

Unlike your home, you can't control what happens in the outside world.

If you've been following along up until this point, you know everything you need to know to make your home a clean, healthy, germ-free sanctuary. But when you leave the walls of your sanctuary and actually exit the house? That's a whole other story.

Unlike your home, you can't control what happens in the outside world. It's full of surfaces you can't clean and air you can't not breathe and people who maybe aren't as obsessed with cleanliness as you are. So let's talk about what you can do to keep yourself safe out there.

Mind Your Stuff

When you leave the safe zone of your home, you aren't just taking your body with you. You're also taking your stuff—like your phone, your briefcase or purse, even the clothes you're wearing. That means you *and* your stuff are going to be exposed to germs. And when you come home, you and your stuff can bring those germs back inside your home.

At the same time, when you go outside, you bring your own germs out into the world and expose other people. So what can you do to keep everybody safe? Before you even leave the house, here are a few things to keep in mind.

1. Don't go out if you're sick. Just don't. It's not good for you, and it's not good for the other people you come into contact with, so if you can avoid it, please do. If you absolutely must, wear a mask and avoid contact with other people as much as possible.

2. If you cough or sneeze, do it into your elbow—and not just because you don't want to spread your germs onto other people. Do it to keep yourself safe. After all, you don't always know where your hand has been. Maybe you touched

something you really don't want near your face, so it's probably wise not to take that chance.

3. Most people don't realize that the places you innocently set your stuff down when you're out and about can be dangerous ... or at least disgusting. How many times have you set your phone or purse on the belt at the grocery store while you unloaded your cart? How often do you think those belts are cleaned? (Hint: not very often!) Now think about the floor of the public restroom, where maybe you set your purse or briefcase. Use wall hooks or ledges you can presanitize, and then set your things there.

4. Do you wear sunglasses, glasses, or readers? If you do, there are probably times when you take them off and set them on a table or other surface ... and then pick them up and put them (and any germs they may have picked up from that surface) back on your face. Not good. If you don't have to take your glasses off, don't. If you do, push them up on your head, or if that's not a good look for you, keep a case handy and put them there.

5. Credit cards and money also carry germs. Paper money carries less than plastic, but it still happens, so sanitize your hands accordingly.

Situations like the ones I described above are the reason I carry a package of sanitizing wipes with me wherever I go. I have used them to wipe down my credit cards, as well as my phone, which has both a protective case and a screen protector. (I also recommend using earbuds for calls, so you don't have to hold your phone next to your face to hear.) I use these sanitizing wipes on most surfaces I encounter—but not all of them. For example, I would not use them on a $2,000 Christian Dior bag. If you try to disinfect leather or suede with a disinfecting wipe, you'll likely kill your purse along with the germs. The good news is: you don't have to. Just make sure to sanitize your hands while you're carrying your briefcase or purse, and when you get home, set it somewhere overnight and leave it alone. I have a table at my back door where I leave my purse when I come in from the garage. By the time I pick it up in the morning, most of the germs are dead.

Getting Around

Once you've left the house and accounted for your stuff, it's time to get where you're going. For most people, this means getting in your car.

Your car is a lot like your house—it's an environment you can easily control and keep germ-free. I keep a pack of wipes in my car for when I need to clean something, although I usually have one in my purse as well, along with hand sanitizer. Note: if you live in a warm climate like I do in Texas, *do not* leave a bottle of hand sanitizer in your car. When they heat up, the chemicals expand, and they can actually explode. Which is a very messy way to sanitize your car.

I clean my car regularly, based on when other people have been in it. This is what I recommend to clean your car for infection prevention:

- If you have a newer car with touchscreens for radios and maps and things like that, clean them by gently wiping them with a microfiber wiper and isopropyl alcohol. Do not ever use glass cleaner or disinfectants on those touchscreens, at least not if you want them to last.

- If you've had people in your car, use disinfectant on a wiper (not sprayed directly on the surface) to clean:

  □ Seatbelt buckles

  □ Door handles

  □ Steering wheel

- I do not spray aerosol disinfectant in my car unless I suspect I have been exposed to something, in which case I spray the car after I get out at home. There is no everyday need to disinfect your car in this way unless you or someone in the car is exposed to an infectious germ.

- If you have child safety seats, do not use harsh chemicals to clean them. There are baby-safe products that are fine for cleaning hard surfaces. The soft parts of car seats can usually be removed, washed in the machine with laundry sanitizer, and air dried.

- I do not recommend using those car cleaners that are designed to leave surfaces like your dashboard or seats looking slick and shiny. It may be pretty, but it's also moist, and moist environments are where germs thrive. When I take my car to the car wash, I always ask them to skip that step, since my goal is to get rid of germs, not give them a place to set up shop!

One last thought on cars—I always sanitize my hands after pumping gas, just because of the sheer amount of bug doo-doo, pollution, and, of course, way too many people touching the handle. If your goal is to stay germ-free, I suggest you do the same.

Using Public Transportation

You can't control everything when you take public transportation, but you can control your immediate environment. If you know you will be riding a bus or train, carry a travel-sized pack of disinfecting wipes with you and wipe down anything that you can. You should also have hand sanitizer with you to kill the germs from anything you might touch that you can't wipe. If you can, roll down your window to encourage air circulation. And of course, avoiding other people and sitting or standing by yourself whenever possible is the safest choice.

If you are using a rideshare service or taxi, roll down the windows if possible to let the fresh air in, and wipe down anything that you need to use. Meaning, if you're going to get out using the door handle, wipe off the door handle. If you're going to pay on one of those little kiosks on the back of the seat in front of you, wipe the keypad down before you have to touch it. If that's not possible, just sanitize your hands afterward.

Out in the World

Once you've arrived at your destination, you'll face a whole new set of infection-avoidance challenges, depending on where you're going. But there are a few general rules. If you have to touch something to open it (like a door) or make it work (like an elevator button), avoid using your fingertips. Use your knuckles, use your elbows, use your foot, your knee; I even use my butt to open doors. If there happens to be an automated door-opening device for the disabled, and you aren't getting in anyone's way, use that.

If you sit at a desk (like at work or school), wipe the surface down with disinfectant, especially if you are in a coworking space. When you go into the coffee room, use a disposable cup, or bring your own mug that you clean yourself.

Finally, even once the COVID-19 pandemic has passed, you should still be cautious about touching other people. Fist or elbow bumps are a perfectly acceptable alternative to handshakes and hugs.

AT THE STORE

If you're shopping at the grocery store, use your own wipes to disinfect the cart and checkout keyboard, since the ones in the store's dispensers are usually dried out. If you don't have wipes, you can also put your hand sanitizer on their dried-out wipes.

AT THE SALON OR SPA

Before you go, check their sanitation protocols, and don't book an appointment anywhere that seems sketchy. Do your due diligence before you go. Try to make your appointment for first thing in the morning, because time is a germ-killer, and most germs will have died overnight. Go during a slow period if possible, so you don't have to wait or be around a lot of people. And of course, take your own wipes and hand sanitizer and don't be afraid to use them.

AT THE GYM

As with salons, check the protocols before you go. Bring your own wipes, because theirs may be dried out, and always wash and sanitize your hands. Don't worry about sanitizing after each and every piece of equipment you use, just be careful to keep your hands away from your face when you're working out.

AT THE DOCTOR OR DENTIST

Sick people go to doctors' offices, so it makes sense that they can be a hotbed for germs. But there are ways to stay safe, and the same techniques will help you at the dentist, the chiropractor, or even your therapist.

Before you go, bring your own pen to use when you check in. Some offices now have separate cups for clean and dirty pens, but if they don't designate, don't take the chance.

The same thing applies to magazines. I'm still amazed at how many doctors' offices have magazines and brochures sitting out in their waiting rooms. If you know you'll be waiting, bring your own book or magazine or play games on your phone, or just zone out.

Some offices now use check-in kiosks, which are convenient, but not always clean. Currently (during the pandemic), a lot of places are adamant about stationing somebody by those kiosks to wipe them down after each patient checks in. However, some smaller offices can't afford to have a staff member spend their entire day just standing by a kiosk, and others may revert back to old practices in the months to come. So, just to be safe, wipe the kiosk down before you use it.

DINING OUT

One of my least-favorite things before the pandemic was the way restaurants cleaned their tables. Somebody would walk around the restaurant with a rag and a bucket of water and use that same rag and dirty water to wipe down every single table, usually for their entire shift. The pandemic changed that, and hopefully, by the time you read this, restaurants will not have reverted back to their old, disgusting ways. Those rags are usually nastier than the table that they're cleaning.

To avoid any germs that may be lurking on your table regardless of how it's cleaned, put your knife and fork either on your napkin or on your plate. You can also wipe the table down yourself with your own wiper and sanitizer, or politely ask the waiter to do it using a fresh wiper or paper towel and disinfectant.

Another tip: if you're at a bar or restaurant where they garnish your drink with a lemon, lime, or some other fruit or vegetable, do not under any circumstance put that piece of fruit or vegetable in your drink. If you're drinking a Mexican beer and you want a lime in it, squeeze the juice into the bottle or glass and throw the fruit away. The reason? Most of these limes, lemons, and other food garnishes are not washed. At all.

Crazy, right?

Finally, I want to talk about gloves. If you see your server wearing them, don't assume that means their hands are germ-free. Because those gloves may be the same pair of gloves that has touched every plate and glass and credit card they've come across all day. Every hospital room has a box of gloves in it so that the doctors and nurses can change their gloves after every patient. Why wouldn't you change your gloves after every diner? It's safer to wash or sanitize hands frequently than to wear the same pair of gloves and transfer the germs. Unfortunately, most restaurants don't operate this way—so be aware.

> **Have you ever heard of a person washing their hands *before* they go to the bathroom? You have now.**

IN THE RESTROOM

Have you ever heard of a person washing their hands *before* they go to the bathroom? You have now. I always wash my hands prior to going to the bathroom for one very good reason—because I don't always know where my hands have been.

In public restrooms, try to use automated features whenever possible—many places have automatic sinks, automatic handwashing and drying machines, even automatic toilet paper and paper towel dispensers. These are always your safest options when you're in a public bathroom.

A lot of restrooms use toilet paper dispensers that cover the toilet paper, which protects it from germs. But sometimes you go into a public restroom and see a big, oversized roll of TP, just sitting there unprotected. When that happens, unroll it two or three times and take the first few sheets off. The same goes for paper towels. If you're in one of those restrooms that keeps a pile of paper towels next to the sink, throw the top one or two away and use the third one. It may not save a tree, but it might save you from getting sick.

Once your hands are clean and dry, use a paper towel or your foot (or even your butt) to open the door when you leave, because not everyone is as conscientious about handwashing as you are.

That should be enough information to keep you safe from germs during most of your everyday activities. In the next chapter, we'll look at how to stay germ-free when you go a little further from home.

CHAPTER 7:

ON THE ROAD

Traveling far from home, especially when you'll be staying somewhere overnight, comes with its own set of challenges. Hotels, motels, and vacation homes and guest rooms are maintained by other people, from the bathroom to the air you breathe to the bed you'll be sleeping on. So what can you do to make sure you're safe in your home away from home? Here are some tips based on what I do when I travel.

Checking In

Whether you're traveling by plane, train, bus, or boat, chances are before you board, you will encounter a security checkpoint. That means you need to take off your watch and your belt and your shoes and put them in a plastic bin alongside everything else you own, so they (and you) can be screened.

So … do you want to know a really disgusting secret? Those bins are *never* washed.

Ever.

So if you have to take your wallet or your phone out, and you want to keep germs off of those items, bring something protective to put them in. I bring a one gallon zip-top food storage bag and put anything that is not in my purse or has to be taken out separately in there. I am not letting anything of mine touch those bins, except shoes, which are never exactly germ-free and should be treated as such.

Getting There

On the bus and train, follow the same rules that apply to short trips. Try to keep the windows open, have hand sanitizer and wipes available, and wipe down everything in your immediate area or that you will touch.

With air travel, there's not an option to open the window, but that's not a problem. Airlines are now circulating their air with outdoor air and running it through HEPA filters. In other words, that air is probably cleaner than the air anywhere else that you could be—including your own home.

Beyond that, my advice is the same for bus and train travel. Wipe down seatbelt buckles, tables, arm rests, and remote controls. You're probably not going to be able to sanitize the little knob you have to pull to open the overhead bin, but don't worry about it. Just sanitize your hands after you've touched it, and keep them sanitized the entire time you're on the plane (or train or bus).

Staying Overnight

People always ask me what's safer when you have to stay overnight—a vacation home or a hotel? The answer is complicated. B&Bs have less traffic, which means they should have less of a viral load. However, hotels have better cleaning protocols than private homes and apartments. You can also request rooms that have been empty longer, although that might not always be an option.

People always ask me what's safer when you have to stay overnight—a vacation home or a hotel? The answer is complicated.

When you know you'll be staying overnight somewhere, make sure to bring some disinfecting wipers and hand sanitizer with you. Once you're inside your room or property, do the following:

- Disinfect the remote, toilet, and sink handles. Yes, it might sound crazy, but you don't really know who has touched them.

- Only use the disposable cups, not the glasses.

- Do not walk barefoot! As a professional, I know hotel carpets are rarely cleaned, and they're pretty gross.

- I remove the bedspread because these are also not cleaned on a regular basis. I make an exception for those white duvet covers that always look perfect with no wrinkles. There's a reason they look like that—they have to be cleaned every time or they look like hell!

- I always decline housekeeping. As I have no doubt made clear, I have my own wipers and I have my own disinfectant. I know which areas I'm going to touch, and I want to make sure that those are as clean as they can be. However, I realize you may be slightly less obsessed, so just follow the previous advice when you go back after your room has been cleaned. And ask housekeeping to leave the window open if possible—a little fresh air never hurts.

- If you're going to use any public areas like an ATM, hot tub, swimming pool, or gym, try to use them at a time when other guests are not. Make sure you wipe down any keyboards, equipment, or whatever you touch, and use hand sanitizer.

Cruises

The COVID-19 pandemic put cruises in the headlines as hotbeds for spreading infection. In reality, however, the real danger people face on cruises isn't from the air or even their fellow passengers—it's from the food and water. Norovirus, which notoriously affects cruises, happens when food or water is contaminated. This tends to happen to food when it's left sitting out ... like at those big, beautiful buffets cruises are famous for.

To avoid a nasty surprise, unless you know how fresh something is or how long it's been sitting out, order off the menu. This applies to buffets at hotels and restaurants too—if you don't know how long it's been there, maybe don't put it in your body. You can also wash any fruit or vegetable that's sitting out with water and agitation, which will remove any pesticides. Finally, and this is going to be a difficult one for sushi-lovers, don't eat any fish that hasn't been thoroughly cooked. Or, if you absolutely must, be very aware of where it comes from and how fresh it is.

Of course, it should go without saying that you should research a cruise line's protocols ahead of time and book your trip with a company with a good record of cleanliness and infection prevention.

RVing

RVing is basically like taking your house on the road. You control your space and everything in it, so there's nothing special you need to do to stay safe inside that space. The main way there are issues with RVs and infection is with water.

When you hook up to get water and dispose of your waste, get some information on where that water comes from to make sure it's safe for whatever you want to use it for. Some RV campgrounds offer nonpotable water for toilets, and if you don't pay attention, you could end up brushing your teeth with something very unpleasant!

Camping

Camping is the safest form of travel there is, from an infection prevention perspective. You're in your own environment, in the fresh air, away from other people.

Bears are a whole other issue. But I'm not an expert on those!

That wraps up my advice for staying safe when you travel. Next, we'll take a brief look at what to do if you need to travel to a specific, and specifically dangerous, destination: the hospital.

CHAPTER 8:

SURVIVING THE HOSPITAL

I probably know more than just about anyone in the world about infection prevention and hospitals. First of all, it's my job. My company contracts with hospitals to help keep their patients and staff healthy and safe from germs. But more importantly, as a person who has suffered from chronic health problems for most of her life, I have spent a crazy amount of time in hospitals, and I know what can go wrong there. As I mentioned in the introduction, my own experiences as a patient are what inspired me to do the work I do.

And guess what? After that three-year period in my twenties when I kept getting infections, after I studied and learned everything I could about preventing them, I never had another. I still haven't. I have, however, been back to the hospital. Several times.

That's why I'm so confident these tips really work.

First of all, if you know you're going to the hospital, before you go, remove any fake fingernails, and take off all of your jewelry. Not because someone might steal them, but because both jewelry and fake nails have teeny, tiny hiding spots for germs. You don't want those anywhere near you while you are in a hospital bed.

While you are staying in the hospital, do not allow any visitors who are sick. I seriously thought about saying, "Don't allow visitors, period," just to be safe, but I don't think you need to go that far. Just make absolutely, positively sure that if a person has so much as a sniffle, they stay home and send a text instead.

No matter how crappy you might feel, make sure you allow the room to be cleaned every day, as there have likely been many people in your room. And if you don't see someone cleaning your room, tell a nurse and ask them to have your room cleaned.

Most importantly, anybody coming into your room needs to wash or sanitize their hands. Including doctors! I still find myself reminding doctors when they walk in. I'll say, "I'm sorry. You just walked in. I didn't see you sanitize your hands. Would you mind?" They'll usually comply.

Every hospital room has a handwashing sink, and every room has boxes of gloves that every person is supposed to use when they come in. But every once in a while, somebody will tell me they just washed their hands or just put their gloves on before they walked in. When that happens, I tell them, "Yes, but you just touched the door handle. So feel free to do it again before you touch my body."

It can be hard to stand up to experts like doctors and nurses, but this is your health we're talking about! You have every right to do whatever you can to protect it.

Finally, when you get home from the hospital, launder all the items you brought home, even if you didn't end up wearing them. Then, disinfect any items that you bring in from the hospital.

If you ever have to go to the hospital, following those tips will keep you safe.

Next, I'll wrap this up by answering a few questions I always get asked that don't exactly fit into any of the categories we've just been through. Meaning, if you're still not 100 percent clear on how to stay safe from infections, don't worry. There's still more to learn!

RANDOM–BUT– IMPORTANT QUESTIONS PEOPLE ASK

B y this point, you should know just about everything you need to know to stay safe from germs. But just in case you still have questions, here are my own, personal FAQs that people ask me all. the. time.

Can You Clean a Mask?

You absolutely can. Put the cloth ones in the laundry with sanitizer. You can even run them through the dryer.

Even better, you can also rewear paper masks even though they're called disposable. I've got some I've worn multiple times—you can tell by how many different shades of lipstick are on them! They're called disposable because they can't be washed, but that doesn't mean they need to be thrown away after a single use. I usually disinfect mine with my hospital-grade disinfectant and then leave them out for a day or two, but you don't work with germs like I do, so you don't need to do that. You don't even have to spray them. You can just let them sit. Almost any germ on a mask will die within a few days. So get a few disposable masks and cycle them around.

What's Better—Sanitizing or Handwashing?

I'm big on handwashing. Part of the reason is that I just do not want that much alcohol on my skin. Because I have to clean them so often, I don't think I'd have any skin left! I prefer washing my hands, and I think it's the better way to go overall. Just make sure you're washing them for twenty seconds, which is two renditions of the "Happy Birthday" song or the "ABC" song, or twenty seconds of whatever song you choose—get creative with it if you want to!

Don't worry about getting the water scalding hot. As long as you're using soap, the germs will die.

Should I Wear Gloves?

Probably not, unless you throw them away and put on a new pair every time you touch something. And if you don't, the germs from everything you touch will be all over those gloves.

How Often Should I Clean My Phone?

I clean my phone at least daily and, on many occasions, more than once in a day. However, I always use a screen saver, because the chemicals I need to disinfect my phone will also ruin my screen. So use a screen saver. Beyond that, I have a trick or hack that I use. If I have my disinfecting stuff nearby and I can put it on a wipe and do it, great. If not, I use those little, tiny packages of eyeglass wipers. I buy those by the ton—I also use them to wipe off my hands if I get something on them that I need cleaned before I can disinfect.

How Safe Are Public Restrooms?

When it comes to public restrooms, my first piece of advice is definitely don't go if you don't have to. If the bathroom is crowded, consider going out and coming back when the line is not so long. If you absolutely have to go, follow the instructions in chapter 6: wash your hands on the way in, and once you use the restroom, don't use your hands to touch anything after you wash them. Use a paper towel to turn off the water and then use it to open the door.

Does UV Light Really Kill Germs?

It does, but only under very specific conditions. The light needs to be intense enough to break a germ apart in a short period of time, and there aren't any personal-use products available that are strong enough to do that. UV lighting is also somewhat damaging to the body—but don't worry. If you follow the rest of the tips in this book, I'm confident you won't need it to keep yourself safe.

What Should I Do if I Think I've Been Exposed?

As an infection prevention professional, I frequently find myself in environments where I am exposed to germs that could make me sick. This is what I do when I suspect I may be vulnerable to something—it is the very same protocol I suggest you follow if you test positive for a virus or know you have been in contact with someone who is sick.

1. Take your clothes off before you enter your home and put them in a plastic bag.

2. Empty the plastic bag of clothes into the washing machine and wash everything with sanitizing laundry detergent.

3. Take a shower.

4. Wear a mask around any other members of your household until you are known to be negative.

5. Wipe down everything you have touched (including your car if you drove) using disposable gloves, masks, and wipers. This is where I spray my car with aerosol disinfectant if I have been exposed to a known case of disease.

6. Put disposable items in a sturdy trash can liner, double tie it, and dispose of it in the trash.

Follow this advice and you should stay safe and germ-free for many healthy years.

And if you have a question I didn't answer in this book, or need help with germ prevention in your home or business, contact me at:

triciaholderman.com
tricia@elitefacsys.com

214-340-0117
10203 Plano Rd. Suite 100
Dallas, TX 75238

Happy germinating,
Tricia